COMMERCIALISM AND JOURNALISM

COMMERCIALISM AND JOURNALISM

HAMILTON HOLT

ISBN: 978-93-5614-393-7

Published: 1909

LECTOR HOUSE LLP
E-MAIL: lectorpublishing@gmail.com

COMMERCIALISM AND JOURNALISM

BY

HAMILTON HOLT
MANAGING EDITOR OF THE INDEPENDENT

1909

Published December 1909

COMMERCIALISM AND JOURNALISM

I N the United States of America, public opinion prevails. It is an axiom of the old political economy, as well as of the new sociology, that no man, or set of men, may with impunity defy public opinion; no law can be enforced contrary to its behests; and even life itself is scarcely worth living without its approbation. Public opinion is the ultimate force that controls the destiny of our democracy.

By common consent we editors are called the "moulders of public opinion." Writing in our easy chairs or making suave speeches over the walnuts and wine, we take scrupulous care to expatiate on this phase of our function. But the real question is: who "moulds" us? for assuredly the hand that moulds the editor moulds the world.

I propose to discuss this evening the ultimate power in control of our journals. And this as you will see implies such vital questions as: Are we editors free to say what we believe? Do we believe what we say? Do we fool all the people some of the time, some of the people all the time, or only ourselves? Is advertising or circulation—profits or popularity—our secret solicitude? Or do we follow faithfully the stern daughter of the voice of God? In short, is journalism a profession or a business?

There are almost as many answers to these questions as there are people to ask them. There are those of us who jubilantly burst into poetry, singing:—

> "Here shall the press the people's rights maintain,"
> Unawed by influence and unbribed by gain."

On the other hand there are some of us quite ready to corroborate from our own experience the confessions of one New York journalist who wrote:—

> There is no such thing in America as an independent press. I am paid for keeping honest opinions out of the paper I am connected with. If I should allow honest opinions to be printed in one issue of my paper, before twenty-four hours my occupation, like Othello's, would be gone. The business of a New York journalist is to distort the truth, to lie outright, to pervert, to vilify, to fawn at the foot of Mammon, and to sell his country and his race for his daily bread. We are the tools or vassals of the rich men behind the scenes. Our time, our talents, our lives, our possibilities, are all the property of other men. We are intellectual prostitutes.

I come to California, therefore, to tell you with all sincerity and candor the real conditions under which we editors do our work, and the forces that help and hinder us in the discharge of our duties to society and to the journals that we control or that control us.

And, first, let me give you succinctly some idea of the magnitude of the industry that we are to discuss. The Census, in its latest bulletin on "Printing and Publishing in the United States," truly and tritely remarks that "Printing occupies a unique position among industries, and in certain aspects excels all others in interest, since the printed page has done more to advance civilization than any other human agency."

But not only does the printing industry excel all other industries in human interest, it excels them in the relative progress it is making. The latest available figures, published in 1905 by the Government, show that the capital invested in the publishing business had doubled in the preceding half decade, despite the fact that publishing is almost unique among industries in the diffusion of its establishments, and in the tenacity with which it still clings to competition in an age of combination. Since 1850 the whole industry has increased over thirty-fold, while all other industries have increased only fifteen-fold. The number of publications in the country, as given, is 21,394. These are capitalized at $239,505,949; they employ 48,781 salaried officers, and 96,857 wage-earners. Their aggregate circulation per issue is 139,939,229; and their aggregate number of copies issued during the year is 10,325,143,188. They consume 2,730,000 tons of paper, manufactured from 100,000 acres of timber. These 21,394 periodicals receive $145,517,591, or 47 per cent of their receipts, from advertising, and $111,298,691, or 36 per cent of the receipts from sales and subscriptions. They are divided into 2452 dailies, of which about one third are issued in the morning and two thirds in the evening; 15,046 weeklies; 2500 monthlies, and a few bi-weeklies, semi-weeklies, quarterlies, etc.

The number of these periodicals has doubled in the last twenty-five years, but at the present moment the monthlies are increasing the fastest, next, the weeklies, and last, the dailies. The dailies issue enough copies to supply every inhabitant of the United States with one every fourth issue, the weeklies with one every other issue, and the monthlies with one copy of each issue for nine months of the year. One third of all these papers are devoted to trade and special interests. The remaining two thirds are devoted to news, politics, and family reading.

Undoubtedly there are many contributing causes which have made the periodical industry grow faster than all other industries of the country. I shall mention only six.

First. The cheapening of the postal, telephone, and telegraph rates, and the introduction of such conveniences as the rural free delivery, so that news and general information can be collected and distributed cheaply and with dispatch.

Second. The introduction of the linotype machines, rapid and multiple presses, and other mechanical devices, which vastly increase the output of every shop that adopts them.

Third. The photo-process of illustrating, which threatens to make wood- and steel-engraving a lost art, and which, on account of its cheapness and attractiveness, has made possible literally thousands of pictured publications that never could have existed before.

Fourth. The growing diffusion of education throughout the country. Our high schools, to say nothing of our colleges and universities, alone graduate 125,000 pupils a year,—all of them fit objects of solicitude to the newsdealer and subscription-agent.

Fifth. The use of wood pulp in the manufacture of paper, by which the largest item in the cost of production has been greatly diminished.

Sixth. The phenomenal growth of advertising.

I shall not attempt to amplify the first five of these causes responsible for the unparalleled growth of periodical literature. But the sixth I shall discuss at some length, for advertising is by all odds the greatest factor in the case.

In olden times the dailies carried only a very little advertising—a few legal notices, an appeal for the return of a strayed cow, or a house for sale. It is only within the past fifty years that advertising as a means of bringing together the producer and consumer began. And, curiously enough, the men who first began to appreciate the immense selling-power that lay in the printed advertisement were "makers" or "fakirs," of patent medicines. The beginning of modern advertising is in fact synchronous with the beginnings of the patent-medicine business.

Even magazine advertising, which is now the most profitable and efficacious of all kinds, did not originate until February, 1860, when "The Atlantic Monthly" printed its first "ad." "Harper's" was founded simply as a medium for selling the books issued from the Franklin Square House, and all advertisements from outsiders were declined. George P. Rowell, the dean of advertising agents, in his amusing autobiography, tells how Harper & Brothers in the early seventies refused an offer of $18,000 from the Howe Sewing Machine Company for a year's use of the last page of the magazine; and Mr. Rowell adds that he had this information from a member of the firm, of whose veracity he had no doubt, though at the same sitting he heard Mr. Harper tell another man about the peculiarities of that section of Long Island where the Harpers originated, assuring him the ague prevailed there to such an extent that all his ancestors had quinine put into their graves to keep the corpses from shaking the sand off.

Before the Civil War it is said that the largest advertisement that ever appeared in a newspaper was given by the E. & T. Fairbanks Company, and published in the New York "Tribune," which charged $3000 for it. Now the twenty large department stores alone of New York City spend, so it is estimated, $4,000,000 a year for advertising, while one Chicago house is said to appropriate $500,000 a year for publicity in order to sell $15,000,000 worth of goods. Those products which are believed to be advertised to the extent of $750,000 or more a year include the Uneeda Biscuits, Royal Baking Powder, Grape Nuts, Force, Fairy Soap and Gold Dust, Swift's Hams and Bacon, the Ralston Mills food-products, Sapolio, Ivory Soap, and Armour's Extract of Beef. The railroads are also very large general advertisers. In 1903 they spent over a million and a quarter dollars in publicity, though this did not include free passes for editors, who, I may parenthetically remark, thanks to the recent Hepburn Act, are now forced to pay their way across the continent just like ordinary American citizens.

It is computed that there are about 20,000 general advertisers in the country and about a million local advertisers. Between the two, $145,517,591 was spent in 1905 to get their products before the public. The Census gives only the totals and does not classify the advertising that appears in the dailies, weeklies, and monthlies. The Rev. Cyrus Townsend Brady, however, has made a very illuminating study[1] of the advertising and circulation conditions of 39 of the leading monthly magazines published in the United States. The first thing that struck his attention was the fact that candid and courteous replies to his requests for information were vouchsafed by all the publishers—quite a contrast to what would have happened from a similar inquiry a generation ago. He next discovered that these 39 magazines, which had an aggregate circulation of over 10,000,000 copies per month, could put a full-page advertisement into the hands of 600,000,000 readers, or seven times the population of the United States, for the astonishingly insignificant sum of $12,000, or for two thousandths of a cent for each reader.

The amount paid by the purchasers of these 39 magazines was $15,000,000, for which they received 36,000 pages of text and pictures, and 25,000 pages of advertisements. Magazine advertisements are better written and better illustrated than the reading matter. This is because they are of no use to the man who pays for their insertion if they do not attract attention, whereas the contributor's interest in his article after its acceptance is mostly nominal. That is, the advertiser must win several thousand readers; the contributor has to win but one editor.

These 39 magazines were found to receive $18,000,000 a year from their advertisements and $15,000,000 from their sales and subscriptions. This shows that in monthly magazines the receipts from advertising and subscriptions are about the same. In weeklies the receipts from advertising are often four times as much as the receipts from sales and subscriptions, while in the dailies the proportion is even greater. The owner of one of the leading evening papers in New York told me that 90 per cent of its total receipts came from advertising. From whatever standpoint you approach the subject, it is the advertisements that are becoming the most important factor in publishing. Indeed, some students in Yale University carried this out to its logical conclusion last autumn by launching a college daily supported wholly by the revenues from advertisements. They put a free copy every morning on the door-mat before each student's room. If it were not for the postal prohibition many dailies and other periodicals would make money by being given away.

Thus you see that if there were no advertisements and the publishers had to rely on their sales and subscriptions for their receipts, the monthlies would have to double their price, and the weeklies and dailies multiply theirs from four to ten times. This advantage to the reading public must certainly be put to the credit of advertising.

The preponderance of advertising over subscription receipts, however, is of comparatively recent occurrence. Thirty years ago the receipts from subscriptions and sales of all the American periodicals exceeded those from advertising by

---

[1] *The Critic*, August, 1905.

$11,000,000; twenty years ago they were about equal; and to-day the advertising exceeds the subscriptions and sales by $35,000,000.

In 1880 the total amount of advertising was equivalent to the expenditure of 78 cents for every inhabitant in the United States; in 1905 it was $1.79. On the other hand, the per capita value of subscriptions has increased hardly at all. The reason of this is the fall of the price of subscriptions. We take more papers but pay less—a cent a copy. Comparatively few buy the New York "Evening Post" for three cents. This is all the more remarkable, because advertising is the most sensitive feature of a most sensitive business and is sure to suffer first in any industrial crisis or depression.

No wonder that the man who realizes the significance of all these figures and the trend disclosed by them is coming to look upon the editorial department of the newspaper as merely a necessary means of giving a literary tone to the publication, thus helping business men get their wares before the proper people. Mr. Trueman A. DeWeese, in his recent significant volume, "Practical Publicity," thinks that this is about what Mr. Curtis, the proprietor of "The Ladies' Home Journal," would say if he ventured to say what he really thought:—

> It is not my primary purpose to edify, entertain, or instruct a million women with poems, stories, and fashion-hints. Mr. Bok may think it is. He is merely the innocent victim of a harmless delusion, and he draws a salary for being deluded. To be frank and confidential with you, "The Ladies' Home Journal" is published expressly for the advertisers. The reason I can put something in the magazines that will catch the artistic eye and make glad the soul of the reader is because a good advertiser finds that it pays to give me $4000 a page, or $6 an agate line, for advertising space.

Yes, the tremendous power of advertising is the most significant thing about modern journalism. It is advertising that has enabled the press to outdistance its old rivals, the pulpit and the platform, and thus become the chief ally of public opinion. It has also economized business by bringing the producer and consumer into more direct contact, and in many cases has actually abolished the middle man and drummer.

As an example of the passing of the salesman, due to advertising, "The Saturday Evening Post" of Philadelphia, in its interesting series of articles on modern advertising exploits, recently told the story of how the N. H. Fairbanks Co. made a test of the relative value of advertising and salesmen. A belt of counties in Illinois were set aside for the experiment, in which the company was selling a certain brand of soap by salesmen and making a fair profit. It was proposed that the identical soap be put up under another brand and advertised in a conservative way in this particular section, and at the same time the salesmen should continue their efforts with the old soap. Within six months the advertised brand was outselling its rival at the rate of $8000 a year.

The Douglas Shoe is another product that is sold entirely by general advertising. So successful has the business become that the company has established retail stores all over the country, in which only men's shoes are sold at $3.50 a pair. Now other shoe-manufacturers have adopted this plan, and in most of our large cities there are several chains of rival retail shoe stores.

But all the advertising is not in the advertising columns. A United States Senator said last winter that, when a bill he introduced in the Senate was up for discussion, the publicity given it through an article he wrote for "The Independent" had more to do with its passage than anything he said in its behalf on the floor of the upper house;—that is, his article was a paying advertisement of the bill. And in mentioning the incident to you, I give "The Independent" a good advertisement.

Universities advertise themselves in many and devious ways—sometimes by the remarkable utterances of their professors, as at Chicago; sometimes by the victories of their athletes, as at Yale; and sometimes by the treatment of their women students, as at Wesleyan. But perhaps the most extraordinary case of university advertising that has come to my attention was when, not so very long ago, a certain state institution of the Middle West bought editorials in the country press at advertising rates for the sole purpose of influencing the state legislature to make them a larger appropriation. In other words the University authorities took money forced from a reluctant legislature to make the legislature give them still more money.

The charitable organizations are now beginning to advertise in the public press for donations, and even churches are falling into line. The Rev. Charles Stelzle, one of the most conspicuous leaders of the Presbyterian Church, has just published a book entitled "Principles of Successful Church Advertising," in which he says:—

> From all parts of the world there come stories of losses in [church] membership, either comparative or actual. In the face of this, dare the Church sit back and leave untried a single method which may win men to Christ, provided that this method be legitimate?... The Church should advertise because of the greatness of its commission, "Go ye into all the world, and preach the Gospel to every creature." To fulfill this command does not mean that Christian men are to confine themselves to the methods of those who first heard the commission.

The question whether advertising pays will never be known in the individual case, for, like marriage, you can't tell till you try it. But in the aggregate, also like marriage, there is no doubt of its value. The tremendous power of persistent advertising to carry an idea of almost any kind into the minds of the people and stamp it there, is amazing. How many "Sunny Jims," for instance, are there in this audience? If there are none, it is singular; for learned judges have referred to him in their decisions, sermons have been preached, and volumes written about him, though it took a million dollars and two years of persistent work to introduce this modern "Mark Tapley" to the public. Have you a little fairy in your home? Do you live in Spotless Town? Do you use any of the 57 varieties? "There's a reason." "That's all." Formerly a speaker used a quotation from the Bible or Shakespeare when he wanted to strike a common chord. Nowadays he works in an allusion to some advertising phrase, and is sure of instant and universal recognition.

The Socialists and other utopian critics, who are supposed to drill to the bed-rock of questions, have looked upon advertising as essentially a parasite upon the production and distribution of wealth. They tell us that in the good time coming, advertising will be relegated to the scrap-heap of outworn social machinery, along with war, race prejudice, millionaires, the lower education of women, and other things of an undesirable nature. This has not been the experience, however, of those "sinister offenders" who have come nearest to the coöperative ownership of wealth in this country—I refer of course to "The Trusts." When the breakfast food trust was formed, one of the chief reasons for the combination was that the rival companies thus hoped to save the cost of advertising that had hitherto been required when they sold their food-stuffs in competition with each other. But they very soon found that their sales fell off after they stopped advertising, and they kept on falling off until the advertising was resumed. This teaches us that the American people have not enough gumption to buy even the staple products they need except through the stimulus of hypnotic suggestion—which is nothing but another name for advertising. Even such a benevolent institution as a great life insurance company could not get much new business on its own merits. If all the money now spent on agents' commissions, advertising, yellow-dog funds, and pa-latial offices were devoted sacredly to the reduction of the rates of insurance, prob-ably fewer rather than more persons would insure. The American people have to pay to be told what is good for them, otherwise they would soon abolish editors, professors, and all the rest of us who get paid for preaching what others practice.

Now while advertising pays the consumer who buys, the advertiser who sells, and the publisher who brings both together, there is a limit to the amount of ad-vertising which can be "carried" by a certain amount of reading matter. In news-papers we see the result of this in the vast Sunday editions, with sometimes fifty or a hundred detachable pages. In the magazines the case is different. Interesting and attractive as magazine advertising has become—it certainly should be so, con-sidering the advertisers pay good money to put it before the people—it is not enough alone to sell a magazine, and when it forms more than half or two thirds of the number the issue becomes too bulky and the value of the advertising pages themselves decreases. In making sandwiches the ham must not be sliced too thin. That necessitates starting a new magazine; and so we find from three to a dozen periodicals issued by the same house, often similar in character and apparently rivals. This accounts for the multiplication of magazines. It is not a yearning for more love stories.

Thus you see advertising has made possible the great complex papers and magazines of the day with their corps of trained editors, reporters, and advertising writers, in numbers and intellectual calibre comparable with the faculty of a good-sized university. Advertising makes it possible to issue a paper far below the cost of manufacturing—all to the benefit of the consumer. So far as I know there is not an important daily, weekly, or monthly in America that can be manufactured at the selling price. But, on the other hand, with the growth of advertising a depart-ment had to be created in every paper for its handling. As advertising still further increased, rival papers competed for it and the professional solicitor became a necessary adjunct of every paper, until now the advertising department is the most important branch of the publication business, for it is the real source of the profits. Because the solicitor seeks the advertiser, and, therefore, is in the position of one asking for favors, he puts himself under obligations to the advertiser, and so in his keenness to bring in revenue for his paper, he is often tempted to ask the aid of the editor in appeasing the advertiser. Thus the advertiser tends to control the policy of the paper.

And this is the explanation of the condition that confronts most publications to-day. By throwing the preponderating weight of commercialism into the scales of production, advertising is at the present moment by far the greatest menace to the disinterested practice of a profession upon which the diffusion of intelligence most largely depends. If journalism is no longer a profession, but a commercial enterprise, it is due to the growth of advertising, and nothing else.

There was a time, not so very long ago, when journalism was on the verge of developing a system of professional ethics, based on other considerations than those of the cash register. Then a Greeley, Bowles, Medill, Dana, or Raymond, with a hand-press and a printer's devil, could start a paper as good as any university consisting of Mark Hopkins, a student, and a log. In those days the universal question was, "What does old Greeley have to say?" because old Greeley was the ultimate source of his own utterances. Imagine the rage he would have flown into if any one had dared insinuate that the advertisers dictated a single sentence in "The Tribune"! But now the advertisers are aggressive. They are becoming organized. They look upon the giving of an advertisement to a publisher as something of a favor, for which they have a right to expect additional courtesies in the news and editorial columns.

Advertising is also responsible for the fact that our papers are no longer organs but organizations. The individuality of the great editor, once supreme, has become less and less a power, till finally it vanishes into mere innocuous anonymity. To show you how far the editor has receded into public obscurity, it is only necessary to try to recall the portrayal of a modern editor in a recent play. Stage lawyers, stage physicians, and stage preachers abound; when you think of them your mind calls up a very definite image. But no one has yet attempted to portray the typical editor, and it is doubtful if the populace would recognize him if he were portrayed, for the modern editor is a mystery.

Despite the editorial impersonality which controls modern newspapers, the editors still touch life in more points than any other class of men. And for this reason, if for no other, it is important to know the limitations under which they work. I leave aside the limitations that come from within the editor himself; for manifestly ignorance, prejudice, venality and the like, in the editor are in no wise different from similar faults in other men.

There are just two temptations, however, peculiar to the editor, that tend to limit his freedom: first, the fear of the advertisers, and second, the fear of the subscribers. The advertisers when offended stop their advertisements; the readers, their subscriptions. The editor who is afraid to offend both must make a colorless paper indeed. He must discuss only those things about which every one agrees or nobody cares. The attitude of such an editor to his readers is, "Gape, sinner, and swallow," and to his advertisers, as Senator Brandegee said at a recent Yale Commencement in regard to a proposed Rockefeller bequest, "Bring on your tainted money." As a rule, the yellows are most in awe of the mob, while the so-called respectables fear the advertising interests.

Now let me take up in some detail the influences brought to bear upon us which tend to make us swerve from the straight and narrow path. I invite your attention first of all to the Press Agent, that indispensable adjunct of all projects that have something to gain or to fear from publicity. I have seen the claim made in print, though doubtless it is a press agent's story, that there are ten thousand press agents in the city of New York,—that is, men and women employed to boom people and enterprises in the papers and magazines. You are familiar with the theatrical press agent, the most harmless, jovial, inventive, and resourceful of his kind. He is the one who writes the articles signed by Grand Opera singers which appear in the magazines. It is he who gets up stories about Miss "Pansy Pinktoes," her milk-baths, the loss of her diamonds, the rich men who follow her. It is he who got for me an interview with a Filipino chief at Coney Island three summers ago, whose unconventional remarks and original philosophy on America and the inhabitants thereof startled me no less than our readers.

When the press agent has no news, he manufactures it. The readers of the New York papers the other day read that a prominent Socialist, who occupied a box in the theatre where a play was given in which Socialism is attacked, stood up and offered to harangue the audience between the acts. The actor who played the rôle of the wicked capitalist came on the stage and invited the audience to vote whether they cared to hear the Socialist or him. The audience thereupon voted both down. But the management the next Sunday evening very kindly offered the use of the stage for a debate on Socialism, to which the leading Socialists and anti-Socialists of the city were invited. The meeting was a great success, and all the reporters in town were present, just as by some singular coincidence they happened to be on the first night.

One of our most successful operatic managers—impressario, I believe, is the more correct appellation—was about to produce the opera of "Salome," which had been taken off the rival stage after its first performance, on the assumption that New York was shocked. The singer was not only to sing the part, if one can sing a Strauss opera, but was also to dance it. Finally, about a week before the opera was produced, a new soprano was engaged to sing another rôle hitherto taken by the prospective Salome. Instantly the dread headlines on all the front pages of the metropolitan press announced that Miss Garden would resign before Madame Cavalieri should sing in any of *her* rôles. Mr. Hammerstein's "eyes twinkled," as the reporters besieged him. He said he guessed he could untangle matters. Out of the kindness of his heart he had thought the rehearsals of "Salome" were too fatiguing for Miss Garden, and so got assistance for her. After a three or four days' operatic war, in which literally columns of printers' ink was shed, the *entente cor-*

diale was resumed, and the song-birds became doves of peace again. The New York "Evening Post" printed the next day an editorial entitled, "Genius in Advertising"; and a week later the opera, or rather the song and dance of "Salome," was given, with seats selling at ten dollars apiece, and "standing room only" signs at the box-office.

This desire for publicity on the part of the histrionic profession goes so far, that often absolute fakes are sent out to the poor, unsuspecting editor. Here is a statement that was printed, let us hope in good faith, in one of the Brooklyn papers not long ago. It referred to the leading lady in a popular stock company.

> Miss S. has a remarkably fine collection of miniatures painted on ivory. Her attention was attracted to them several years ago by a miniature of one of her ancestors, painted by Edward Greene Malbone, which came into her possession. The delicate quality of the painter's art that was of necessity lavished upon the ivory pleased her as an amateur and she began to collect. Miss S. has haunted the antique shops of Manhattan and Brooklyn during the few leisure moments that came to her, in her search after miniatures. She now owns something like one hundred examples of famous miniatures. One of her greatest treasures is a portrait of John Dray, by that master-painter of miniatures, Richard Cosway.

The publication of this article brought such a number of requests from the friends of Miss S. to see her collection, that the ingenious press agent was obliged to invent and publish another fabrication—this time of a midnight robbery in which the collection disappeared. This shameless story was told me by the press agent himself, and he gave me from his scrap-book the fake clipping I have just read.

Similarly the imitation riots, and protests from delegations of negroes, where Thomas Dixon's Ku-Klux play, "The Clansman," was to be produced, were often due to the initiative of the enterprising press agent—at least so he told me.

I would not have you think, however, that the press bureau is not in many instances a perfectly legitimate institution, and cannot be used with all propriety by religious, reform, political, and other organizations. The woman's suffrage movement, for instance, has a well-equipped and organized bureau; while the two great political parties during campaign times have sent out for many years news-articles and editorials of great value to the country and partisan press.

Perhaps the most efficacious press bureau of the legitimate kind is that of the Christian Scientists. Every time an editor prints anything derogatory to the Rev. Mary Baker G. Eddy, or her influential cult, a suave and professionally happy gentleman immediately sends his card into the sanctum, and, holding the offensive clipping in one hand, together with a brief and well-written reply, says with the utmost courtesy:—

> "Inasmuch, my good sir, as you deemed it worth while to devote so much of your valuable space to spreading broadcast before your intelligent audience an error about Christian Science,

I feel sure that your sense of justice will make plain to you the privilege of giving us space to demonstrate the real truth of the matter."

To the editor with a conscience—and some of us still have the vestiges of one—this is a hard argument to evade; and as a result Christian Science gets twice as much notice in the papers as it would were there no smiling press agent to follow up every unfavorable reference, no matter how obscure the publication. The next time the editor wants to point a jest at the expense of Christian Science, he thinks twice and then substitutes some other cause that does not employ an editorial rectifier.

But perhaps the best use of a publicity bureau was made recently by the street-railway company of Roanoke, Virginia, and the water company of Scranton, Pennsylvania. Both of these companies had become very unpopular, one as a result of poor street-car service, and the other on account of a typhoid epidemic supposed to have been started from the pollution of the company's reservoir. Both companies appropriated a good sum of money, hired a press agent, and bought advertising space in the local papers every day for a month or more. These advertisements gave the companies' side of the case with such candor and convincing fairness that they soon became the talk of the town, personal letters were written to the papers about them, and the hostility toward them very quickly turned to a feeling of good-will. It pays to take the public into your confidence.

And now the staid "Rail-Road Age-Gazette" has sounded the call for a great press agent to arise and stem the growing public hostility to the railroads. The "Age-Gazette" did not use the phrase "press agent," as the appellation has not as yet come into its full dignity. It employed the more euphonious term "Railroad Diplomatist." Still, high-sounding titles have their use, as when some of my brother editors call their "reporters" "Special Commissioners," and their foreign correspondents "Journalistic Ambassadors."

We had a Peace and Arbitration Congress in New York two years ago. Being chairman of the Press Committee, I employed a firm of press agents to get for us the maximum amount of publicity. As a result we received over ten thousand clippings from the papers of the United States alone. I do not mean to claim that the Congress would not have been extensively noticed without the deft work of the agents; but they unquestionably helped a great deal. The newspapers welcome them when they represent such well-known philanthropic institutions as the Peace Society, the Society for Prevention of Cruelty to Animals, and the People's Institute, because the copy they "turn in" requires little or no further editing before it is sent to the printer. But when they are employed to promote financial ventures, wars on labor unions, anti-municipal ownership campaigns, or other private and class interests, then the editors discount what they provide and they actually do more harm than good to the cause they are intended to promote.

Press agents, however, are sometimes enabled to get illegitimate matter into our best papers. I recall to your memory the reports favorable to the companies sent out during the great insurance investigations in New York. "Collier's" has told the whole story.[2] One of the agents employed testified on the witness-stand that a great insurance company agreed to pay a dollar a line for what he could get into the papers. He made his own arrangements with the journals that took his stuff, and the difference between the price he had to pay and the dollar a line he got from the insurance company was to be his private rake-off. He succeeded in securing the publication of six dispatches of about two hundred and fifty words, in such well-known newspapers as the St. Paul "Pioneer Press," the Boston "Herald," the Toledo "Blade," the Buffalo "Courier," the Florida "Times-Union," the Atlanta "Constitution," and the Wilmington "News." It is only fair to state, however, that there was nothing in the evidence to show whether the papers went into the arrangement on a business basis, or were fooled into thinking the dispatches they published were genuine reports of the proceedings before the committee.

Examples of the use of press agents for both legitimate and illegitimate purposes could be extended almost indefinitely. The Standard Oil Company, I understand, now issues all its manifestoes to the public through a trained press-representative; and the fight against Messrs. Gompers, Mitchell, and Morrison, in the Buck Stove controversy, was conducted with the aid of a press bureau, as one of the lawyers in the case informed me. Whenever such a question comes before the people as the choice between the Nicaragua and Panama routes for the interoceanic canal, a press bureau is usually an important factor in the campaign. The big navy craze and the Japan war cry can hardly be accounted for except on the theory that it has been for somebody's interest to agitate them through the press. Whenever the Naval appropriation bill comes before Congress, the Far-Eastern war-clouds threaten in thousands of newspaper sanctums, while all of us shudder at the danger of war, for the benefit of ordnance manufacturers, battleship builders, and every incipient "Fighting Bob" who hopes some day to command another American Armada on its gastronomic voyage around the world.

Fortunately none of our papers are subsidized by the government itself, as is so often the case with the semi-official organs of Europe. Nor are any of our papers directly in the pay of foreign governments, though the espousal of the infamous reactionary régime in Russia by some of them is at least open to suspicion. The danger of manufactured public opinion in this country comes not from governments. Even the political parties are losing the allegiance of the press. The days when the Republican organs told the people the worst Republican was better than the best Democrat, and the Democratic papers said the same about the Republicans, have happily passed, never to return again, though the spirit still lingers in the organs of the Socialist, Populist, and Prohibition parties. The growth of the great politically-independent press is one of the most hopeful signs of the times.

But we have only jumped out of the frying-pan of politics into the fire of commercialism, and the fight of the future will therefore be to extricate ourselves from the fetters of commercialism, just as we have already broken away from the bonds of party politics.

But the press agent has come to stay. Indeed, his business has now assumed such proportions that the profession of anti-press agent will doubtless soon come

[2] *Collier's*, Nov. 11, 1905.

into existence. I know already of one gentleman in New York whose aid has been invoked when people want things kept out of the papers. On more than one occasion he has prevented good spicy bits of scandal from seeing the light; though in his case I can aver that it was his personal influence with the editors, rather than any improper lubricant, that kept the papers silent.

Now let me turn from the press agent to the advertiser as a twister of editorial opinion. Here let me say at once, and with all emphasis, that the vast majority of advertisements are not only honest but dependable. Leaving out of account a few stock phrases which deceive nobody, such as "the most for the money," "the cheapest in the market," etc., what is said about the goods to be sold is not in the least overdrawn. I have taken the pains to go over the advertising columns of the leading papers and periodicals of New York during the month of February, and, with the exception of a few medical, financial, and perhaps real-estate advertisements, I could find absolutely nothing that on the face of it seemed fraudulent, and very little that was misleading. The advertisers have at last come to realize that for the long run, whatever the rule may be for the short run, it does not pay to overstate the qualities of their merchandise. You can now order your purchases by mail from the advertising pages of any reputable publication about as safely as over the counter of a store. At all events the phenomenal growth of the mail-order houses and their sales through advertising, lend strength to this opinion. On the 15th of March, 1909, a single Chicago mail-order house sent to the Post Office six million catalogues, weighing four hundred and fifty tons, and all were to be distributed within a week.

Many periodicals now claim that they will not take advertisements that look fraudulent or even misleading. Some papers, like the London "Times," have a guaranteed list of advertisements which they have investigated and vouch for, though naturally the advertisers have to pay extra for the guarantee.

"The Sunday School Times" printed, several weeks ago, a long list of secular papers that were "going dry," as so many of our Southern states. The fact that our best periodicals no longer accept liquor advertisements is another one of the encouraging signs of the coming of the new journalism.

The vigorous fight that "The Ladies' Home Journal" and "Collier's" waged against the patent-medicine concerns is too fresh in the public memory to need recounting here. The two pictures printed cheek by jowl in "The Ladies' Home Journal,"—one, of the tombstone above the mortal remains of Lydia E. Pinkham, whose inscription showed that she had been dead since 1883, and the other an advertisement representing Lydia in 1905, sitting in her laboratory at Lynn, Massachusetts, engrossed in assuaging the sufferings of ailing womanhood,—these are eloquent of the type of fraud perpetrated through the press upon a gullible public.

Similarly, in the negro papers the favorite advertisements are those that claim to straighten kinky hair and bleach complexions—all fakes, of course. Perhaps the most fraudulent advertisements, however, are those which purpose to sell mines in Brazil, Mexico, Alaska, or wherever else the investor is unlikely to go. These offer their shares often as low as ten cents each, and guarantee fabulous profits. I have a college classmate who is extensively interested in Mexican mines, and he tells me that literally 99 per cent of all the mining companies that float their shares through advertisements are pure, or rather impure, swindles. I am not in the least surprised, for I know how many letters come to a financial editor from the dupes of these slick mine promoters, asking advice as to how they can get their money back.

The most demoralizing advertisements are those paid for by loan-sharks, clairvoyants, medical quacks, and the votaries of vice. The New York "Herald" has recently stopped printing its vicious personals. It also refuses fortune-tellers the hospitality of its columns, though it is not so squeamish in regard to loan-agencies and patent medicines. How many papers still publish the advertisement of Mrs. Laudanum's soothing syrup for babies? When you remember that the proprietary medicine concerns have been accustomed to spend forty million dollars a year, which is distributed among the papers of the land, you can see that it requires considerable financial independence for a publisher to forego a taste of their patronage.

It is a curious fact that, aside from the country weeklies, the papers most plentifully besprinkled with medical advertisements are the yellow journals, the religious weeklies, the socialistic and other propaganda organs, and in general those which preach most vociferously reform and the brotherhood of man.

The danger from the advertising columns is not, as I have said, that the advertisements misrepresent the goods, but that the terms on which they are solicited tend to commercialize the whole tone of the paper and make the editor afraid to say what he believes. The advertiser is coming more and more to look on his patronage as a favor, and he seldom hesitates to withdraw his advertisement if anything appears that may injure his business or interfere with his personal fad or political ambition.

Let me give you some examples of the withdrawal of advertisements to punish too daring and independent editors.

A few weeks ago the paper which, in my opinion, has the ablest editorial page in the country lost some very valuable musical advertising because it had published letters of a decidedly compromising nature, written by a man high in the musical world to a lady who was suing him for damages. Another paper, which many consider the brightest in America, discharged its dramatic critic after a theatrical firm had taken out all their advertising. But strange to say, as soon as a new critic was engaged, the advertising was forthwith resumed. I refrain from giving the name of this newspaper because one brave and witty little weekly published the story with names and dates, and is now being sued for libel.

"Life" states that in Cincinnati, lately, every theatrical advertisement in all other newspapers carried this line:—

"We do not advertise in 'The Times-Star.'"

The paralyzing power of advertising is again exemplified in the case of a New York evening paper which was so much interested in the popularization of bicycles that it organized the first bicycle parade ever held in the city. Just before the day of the parade, however, it printed an article telling the people that it cost only some fifteen or twenty dollars to manufacture bicycles that sold at from seventy-five to one hundred and twenty-five dollars. Instantly all the bicycle advertising was withdrawn, and the paper lost thousands of dollars.

The New York "Evening Post" some years ago offended the department stores by some utterance it made about the tariff, and they withdrew their advertising. The "Evening Post," instead of quietly backing down, started in to fight single-handed, calling on the public for aid. The personal friends of the editor, Mr. Godkin, and a few loyal readers rallied to its support, and threatened to boycott the stores. But the public as a whole and all the "Post's" esteemed contemporaries, as might have been anticipated, enjoyed the conflict from a safe distance and minded their own business. The department stores not only refused to make terms, but in some instances carried the war into the enemy's territory by stopping the credit accounts of those customers who took the "Post's" side. It was only after a very great financial loss and many years of estrangement, that most of the stores came back to the "Post," and it was long before the old relations of cordiality were entirely reëstablished.

The department stores are seldom or never referred to unfavorably by the New York papers. When an elevator falls down in an office-building and somebody is injured, the headlines ring to heaven. A similar catastrophe in a department store is considered of hardly sufficient human interest to publish. The name and shame of a woman caught shoplifting in a department store can seldom be kept out of the papers. A department store caught overworking and underpaying its sales-girls—well, that is of no public concern. One of the most striking articles I ever printed recounted the experiences of a sales-girl in one of New York's department stores, yet it was unnoticed by the New York papers, which are quick enough to republish and comment on such articles when we print them, as "Graft in Panama," "Peonage in Georgia," or "Race-Prejudice in California."

Four years ago, in our annual vacation number, we advised our readers to go back to their boyhood village, buy the old homestead, and take a vacation on the farm, abjuring the summer hotels with their temptations to spend money, their vapidities and artificialities, manufactured lovers' lanes, and old cats on the piazza. This so offended a few hotels that they have never since advertised in "The Independent." I will not tell you their names, but you can find out by noticing what hotels are not represented in our advertising pages.

Three years ago I printed the life-story of a girl then on strike in a factory. It was a simple, straightforward autobiography, giving the employés' side of the case. Although we printed subsequently—as we are always glad to do—a statement from the company giving their side of the controversy, we must still be on their "We Don't Patronize" list, judging by the amount of advertising with which they have since favored us. Other papers have suffered still more, I understand, from the same factory.

The great book-publishing firms are about the only class of advertisers I know of who do not directly or indirectly seem to object to have their wares damned in the editorial pages. Whether they have attained more than other men to the Christian ideal of turning the other cheek; whether they think that nobody pays any attention to a scathing book-review, or whether they hold that the "best seller" is the offspring of hostile criticism, I do not know. But again and again we denounce books in our literary department that the publishers pay good money to praise in the advertising pages of the same issue. I know of only one prominent publishing firm which is an exception to this rule in that it sometimes attempts to influence the reviews of its books by means of its patronage.

But with the small book-houses this happy relationship does not always exist. It would surprise you to know how many of them badger and threaten us. Some, I understand, have a rule not to advertise where their books are not indiscriminately puffed. It is a poor Maxim, however, that won't shoot both ways; for I am sorry to report that some papers adopt the equally bad rule of not reviewing the books of these firms who do not keep an advertising account with them.

I once dined at a public banquet where the guests were both whites and negroes, and made some harmless and well-meaning remarks. A Philadelphia advertiser subsequently said he would never do business with a paper that employed such an editor.

Last year an insurance company withdrew its advertising from the columns of a great weekly because it repeated a disagreeable truth about one of its directors.

Recently San Francisco has gone through one of the most important struggles for civic betterment ever waged in an American city. The whole nation stood at attention. The issue was clear and unequivocal. The story of how San Francisco was redeeming her fair name, as every newspaper man knows, was sensational enough to be featured day by day on the front pages of every great paper in the land. The Eastern dailies started in bravely enough, but soon cut down their reports until they became so meagre and inadequate as to cause people in the East to surmise that some influence hostile to the prosecution had poisoned the sources of their information.

The Archbold letters, given to the press by Mr. Hearst in the late campaign, are further examples of commercialism in journalism. How the Standard Oil Company sent its certificates of deposit and giant subscriptions to sundry editors and public-opinion promoters, and how a member of Congress from the great state of Pennsylvania actually suggested to Mr. Archbold that it might be a good plan to obtain "a permanent and healthy control" of that very fountain-head of publicity,—the Associated Press,—these sinister transactions and suggestions have been so fully discussed as to need no further comment from me.

From the standpoint of journalistic ethics, the only thing more reprehensible than selling your opinions is offering them for sale. This is editorial prostitution. The mere getting out of winter-resort numbers, automobile numbers, financial numbers, and Alaska-Yukon-Pacific Exposition numbers is not at all to be condemned, though the motive may be commercial, as the swollen advertising pages in such special numbers attest.

But what shall we suspect when a paper which claims a million readers devotes a long editorial to praising a poor play, and then in a subsequent issue there appears a full-page advertisement of that play? What does it mean when not a single Denver paper publishes a line about three nefarious telephone bills before the Colorado Legislature? And what shall we think of a certain daily whose editor recently told me that there was on his desk a list three feet long of names of prominent people who were not to be mentioned in his paper either favorably or unfavorably?

But direct bribe-giving and bribe-taking are, as I have said, very rare. Such a procedure is too crude. If you should get up some palpable advertisement disguised as news, and send it around to the leading papers asking them to put it in as reading matter, and send you the bill, expecting them to swallow the bait, you would be disappointed. It is more likely to be done in another way. A financier invites an editor to go with him on a cruise in his private yacht to the West Indies, or offers to let him in on the ground floor in some commercial undertaking. Then, after the editor is under obligations, favors are asked and the editor is enmeshed.

Although I have said much about the sordid side of journalism, and the temptations that we editors have to meet in one form or another, I do not want you to think that the profession or trade of journalism offers no scope for the highest moral and intellectual attainments. I have dwelt thus long on the seamy side of our profession because there is a seamy side, and I believe it does good occasionally to discuss it with frankness. The first step in correcting an evil is to acknowledge its existence. Were the title of this lecture "Journalism and Progress," or "The Leadership of the Press," I could have told a far different and rosier, though a no less true story.

But, as I approach my conclusion, let me give you some more pleasing examples of the better side of "Commercialism and Journalism."

George Jones, the late owner of the New York "Times," when that paper made its historic fight against the Tweed Ring, was offered five million dollars by "Slippery Dick" Connolly, one of the gang, and an officer of the city government, if he would sell the "Times," which was then not worth over a million. Mr. Jones said afterwards, "The devil will never make a higher bid for me than that." Yet he declined the bribe without a tremor. A certain religious weekly lost a hundred thousand dollars for refusing to take patent-medicine advertisements—probably ten times what the paper was worth. "Everybody's Magazine," and many others of its class, refuse every kind of questionable advertising.

Many editors and publishers scrupulously eschew politics, lest obligations be incurred that might limit their opportunities for public service. Some will not even accept dinner invitations when the motive is known to be the expectation of a *quid pro quo*.

Perhaps one of the few disagreeable things a conscientious editor cannot hope to avoid is the necessity of denouncing his personal friends. Yet this must be done again and again. Indeed, there are thousands of editors to-day who will not hesitate a moment to espouse the unpopular cause, though they know it will endanger their advertising receipts and subscription list.

"The Independent," for instance, could undoubtedly build up a great circulation in the South among white people if we could only cease expressing our disapproval of the way they mistreat their colored brothers. But we consider it a duty to champion a race, who, through no fault of their own, have been placed among us, and whom few papers, statesmen, or philanthropists feel called upon to treat as friends.

There is a limit, of course, to the length to which a paper can go in defying its constituency, whether advertisers or subscribers. Manifestly a paper cannot be published without their support. But there are times when an editor must defy them, even if it spells ruin to himself and bankruptcy to the paper. It is rarely necessary, however, to go to such an extremity as suicide. The rule would seem to be—and I think it can be defended on all ethical grounds—that under no circumstances should an editor tell what he knows to be false, or urge measures he believes to be harmful. This is a far different thing from telling all the truth all of the time, or urging all the measures he regards as good for mankind in season and out. That is the attitude of the irreconcilable, and the irreconcilable is as ineffectual in journalism as he is in church or state. Thus "The Ladies' Home Journal" has not as yet taken any part in furthering the great woman's suffrage movement which is sweeping over the world, and which ought to, but nevertheless does not, interest most American women. From Mr. Bok's point of view this policy of silence is quite right, and the only one doubtless consistent with the great circulation of his magazine. A periodical which wants a million readers must adhere strictly to the conventions if it would keep up its reputation as a safe guide for the multitude. This may not be the ideal form of leadership, but it is common sense, which is, perhaps, more to be desired. "Ed" Howe, the editor of "The Atchison Globe," the paper which gets closer to the people than any other in America, evidently admires this theory of editing, for he confesses, "When perplexities beset me and troubles thicken, I stop and ask myself what would Edward Bok have me do, and then all my difficulties dissolve."

Despite the sinister influences that tend to limit the freedom of editors and taint the news, the efficiency, accuracy, and ability of the American press were never on such a high plane of excellence as they are to-day. The celerity with which news is gathered, written, transmitted, edited, published, and served on millions of breakfast-tables every morning in the year is one of the wonders of the age. When great events happen, especially of a dramatic nature, we see newspapers at their best. Witness the recent wreck of the steamship Republic. Only a few wireless dispatches were sent out by the heroic Binns during the first few hours, and yet every paper the next morning had columns about the disaster, all written without padding, inaccuracy, or disproportion. Also recall the way the press handled the recent Witla kidnaping case. Within twenty-four hours every newspaper reader in the United States was apprised of the crime in all its details, and in most cases the photograph of the little boy was reproduced.

It is the gathering of the less important news of the day, however, where reporting has deteriorated, and yellow journalism is largely responsible for this.

Yellow journalism is a matter of typography and theatrics. The most sensational, and often the most unimportant, news is featured with big type, colored inks, diagrams, and illustrations. "A laugh or tear in every line" is the motto above the desk of the copy editor. The dotted line showing the route taken by the beautiful housemaid as she falls out of the tenth-story window to the street below adds a thrill of the yellow "write up." The two prime requisites for an ideal yellow newspaper, as that prince of yellow editors, Arthur Brisbane, once told me, are sport for the men and love for the women; and as the Hearst papers have secured their great circulation by putting in practice this discovery, we find the other papers are consciously or unconsciously copying them. A typographical revolution has thus been brought about, as well as a general deterioration of reporting. Even in papers of the highest character an over-indulgence in headlines is coming into vogue, while the reporter is allowed too often to treat the unimportant and most personal events in a picturesque or facetious way without regard to truthfulness. On a lecture trip West last winter, a reporter of one of the most respectable and influential papers in the country asked if I was going to attack anybody in my speech, or say anything that would "stir up the mud." When I said I hoped not, he replied that it would not be necessary for him to attend the lecture. "Just give me the title, and the first and last sentences," said he, "and I'll write up an account of it at my desk in the office."

Sometimes, by this method of reporting, a serious injury is done to the individual. A reporter on the New York "Times" wrote up last winter a sensational account of the marriage of the head worker of the University Settlement on the East Side to a young leader of one of the girls' classes. The marriage was performed by one of the officers of the Society of Ethical Culture, who are expressly authorized by the New York legislature to officiate on such occasions. And yet the reporter called the marriage an "ethical" one, putting the word "ethical" in quotation marks and also the word "Mrs.," to which the bride was morally and legally entitled, implying that the marriage was irregular, and indicated a tendency towards free love. Though many letters of protest were written to the "Times" about this, the "Times" made no editorial apology for a breach of journalistic ethics, which should have cost the reporter who wrote the article and probably the managing editor who passed it their positions.

It is this lack of sense of the fitness of things that would make the average reporter scribble away for dear life, if, when the President's message on the tariff was being read in Congress, a large black cat had happened to walk up the aisle of the House and jumped on the back of Speaker Cannon. Such an occurrence, I venture to say, would have commanded more space in the next morning's papers than any pearls cast before Congress by the President in his message.

The yellows, however, despite their "night special" editions issued before nine o'clock in the morning, their fake pictures and fake sensations, have come to stay. They serve yellow people. Formerly the masses had to choose between such papers as "The Atlantic Monthly," "The Nation," the New York "Tribune," and nothing. No wonder they chose nothing. In the yellow press they now have their own champion,—a press that serves them, represents them, leads them, and exploits them, as Tammany Hall does its constituency. Of course they give it their suffrage. The hopeful thing is that yellow readers don't stay yellow always. When a man begins to read he is apt to think. When he begins to think there is no telling where he will end,—maybe by reading the London "Times" or the "Edinburgh Review." In New York the yellow papers, while they still have an enormous circulation, are losing their influence as a political and moral force. Evidently as soon as yellow people begin to use their wits they first apply them to the yellow journals.

The daily newspapers, however, both yellow and white, like natural monopolies, are public necessities. The people must have the news, and therefore, the predatory interests, whether political or financial, have been quick to get control of the people's necessity. "Read the comments on the Payne Tariff Bill," says the "Philadelphia North American" in its issue of March 20, "and every sane, well-informed American discounts the comment of the Boston papers regarding raw and unfinished materials that affect the factories of New England. Most of the Philadelphia criticism counts for no more than what New Orleans says of sugar, or Pittsburg of steel, or San Francisco of fruits, or Chicago of packing-house products. And it is common knowledge that what almost every big New York paper says is an echo of Wall Street."

The weeklies and monthlies, however, are not, like the dailies, necessities. They have to attract by their merits alone. They must at all hazards therefore retain the people's confidence in their integrity, enterprise, and leadership. Whether this be the true explanation or not, there is at least no doubt that the moral power of the American periodical press has been transferred from the dailies to the monthlies and weeklies. The monthlies and weeklies have also the advantage of being national in circulation instead of local, and therefore less subject to local and personal influence. They are also preserved, bound or unbound, and not thrown away on the day of publication like the daily paper. At all events, the weeklies and monthlies have been the pioneers and prime movers in the great moral renaissance now dawning in America. Moral strife always brings out moral leaders. Where will you find in the daily press to-day twenty editors to compare with Richard Watson Gilder and Robert Underwood Johnson, of "The Century," Henry M. Alden and George Harvey, of "Harper's," Ray Stannard Baker and Ida M. Tarbell, of "The American," Lyman Abbott and Theodore Roosevelt, of "The Outlook," Walter Page, of "The World's Work," Albert Shaw, of the "Review of Reviews," Paul E. More, of "The Nation," S. S. McClure, of "McClure's," Erman Ridgway, of "Everybody's," Bliss Perry, of "The Atlantic Monthly," Norman Hapgood, of "Collier's," Edward Bok, of "The Ladies' Home Journal," George H. Lorimer, of the "Saturday Evening Post," Robert M. La Follette, of "La Follette's," William J. Bryan, of "The Commoner," or Shailer Matthews, of "The World To-day"? These are the men—and there are more, too, I might name—who came forward with their touch upon the pulse of the nation when the day of the daily newspaper as a leader of enlightened public opinion had waned. As a Philadelphia daily has admitted, "A vacuum had been created. They filled it."

Let me quote from a recent editorial,[3] which seems to sum up this transfor-

---

[3] *The Independent*, Oct. 1, 1908.

mation most clearly:—

> "The modern American magazines have now fallen heir to the power exerted formerly by pulpit, lyceum, parliamentary debates, and daily newspapers in the moulding of public opinion, the development of new issues, and dissemination of information bearing on current questions. The newspapers, while they have become more efficient as newspapers, that is, more timely, more comprehensive, more even-handed, more detailed, and, on the whole, more accurate, have relinquished, or at least subordinated, the purpose of their founders, which was generally to make people think with the editor and do what he wanted them to do. The editorials, once the most important feature of a daily paper, are rarely so now. They have become in many cases mere casual comment, in some have been altogether eliminated, in others so neutralized and inoffensive that a man who had bought a certain daily for a year might be puzzled if you asked him its political, religious, and sociological views. He would not be in doubt if asked what his favorite magazine was trying to accomplish in the world. Unless it is a mere periodical of amusement it is likely to have a definite purpose, even though it be nothing more than opposition to some other magazine. If a magazine attacks Mrs. Eddy, another gallantly rushes to her defense. If one gets to seeing things at night, the other becomes anti-spirituous. If the first acquires the muck-raking habit, the complementary organ publishes an 'Uplift Number' that oozes optimism from every paragraph. The modern editor does not sit in his easy-chair, writing essays and sorting over the manuscripts that are sent in by his contributors. He goes hunting for things. The magazine staff is coming to be a group of specialists of similar views, but diverse talents, who are assigned to work up a particular subject, perhaps a year or two before anything is published, and who spend that time in travel and research among the printed and living sources of information."

Now my conclusion of the whole question under discussion is this: While commercialism is at present the greatest menace to the freedom of the press, just as it is to the freedom of the Church and the University, yet commercialism as it develops carries within itself the germ of its own destruction. For no sooner is its blighting influence felt and recognized than all the moral forces in the community are put in motion to accomplish its overthrow, and as the monthlies and weeklies have thrived by fighting commercialism, so it is reasonable to suppose that the dailies will regain their editorial influence when they adopt the same attitude.

I know of only four ways to hasten the time when commercialism will cease to be a reproach to our papers.

First. The papers can devote themselves to getting so extensive a circulation that they can ignore the clamor of the advertisers. But this implies a certain truckling to popularity, and the best editors will chafe under such restrictions.

Second. The papers can become endowed. That others have thought of this before, Mr. Andrew Carnegie can doubtless testify. There would be many advantages, however, of having several great endowed papers in the country. The same arguments that favor endowed theatres or universities apply equally to papers. We need some papers that can say what ought to be said irrespective of anybody and everybody, and which can serve as examples to other papers not so fortunately circumstanced. But manifestly the periodical industry as a whole is much too large to be endowed, and the few papers that may be endowed by private capital, or by the Government, would have only a limited influence on the industry as a whole. Our government now publishes a weekly paper in Panama, which takes no advertisements, and is furnished free to every government employee on the Isthmus. It is a model paper in many respects, but manifestly its example is not apt to be followed extensively before the dawn of the Coöperative Commonwealth. It may be that the practice newspapers conducted by the schools of journalism connected with our great universities will raise the standard by making their chief object the publication of accurate and reliable news.

Third. The papers can combine in a sort of trust. Take the Theatrical Syndicate, for instance, whose theatres could not be kept open a week without newspaper publicity. The Theatrical Syndicate's policy seems to be to single out any paper that becomes too critical and give it an absent-advertisement treatment. At the present moment this medicine is being prescribed in several of our large cities. But let all the publishers form a publishers' trade union as it were, and whenever an advertisement is withdrawn, appoint a committee of investigation, and if the committee reports that the withdrawal of the advertisement was done for any improper reason, then let all the papers refuse to print an advertisement of the play, or allow their critics to mention it until the matter is satisfactorily adjusted. This would bring the advertisers to their knees in a moment.

The papers have the whip hand if they will only combine, but they are all so jealous of one another that probably any real combination is a long way off. Still there are indications of a gentleman's agreement in the air, for all other interests are combining and they will be forced to follow suit.

And what will the public do then, poor thing? A newspaper trust will certainly be as inimical to the public welfare as any other combination doing business in the fear of the Sherman law. Indeed it would be more dangerous, for a periodical trust would practically control the diffusion of intelligence, and that no self-respecting democracy would or should allow. But this is borrowing trouble from the future.

Fourth and last. We come back to the old, old remedy, which if sincerely applied would solve most all the ills of society. I refer to personal integrity, to character. Despite what may be said to the contrary, integrity is the only thing in the newspaper profession, as in life itself, that really counts.

The great journalists of the past, whatever their personal idiosyncrasies, have all been men of integrity; the great journalists of to-day are of the same sterling mould; and the journalistic giants of to-morrow—and the journalists of the future will be giants—must also be men of inflexible character.

There has never been a time in all history when so many and so important things were waiting to be done as to-day. The newest school of sociology tells us that the human race in its spiral progress onward and upward through sweat and blood, misery and strife, has at last reached the point where, emerging from the control of the blind forces of an inexorable environment, it is about to take its destiny into its own control and actually shape its future. From now on, evolution is to be a psychical rather than a physical process. The world is on the threshold of a new era. We see the first faint dawn of universal peace and of the brotherhood of man.

Fortunate that editor whose privilege it is to share in pointing out the way.

Lector House believes that a society develops through a two-fold approach of continuous learning and adaptation, which is derived from the study of classic literary works spread across the historic timeline of literature records. Therefore, we aim at reviving, repairing and redeveloping all those inaccessible or damaged but historically as well as culturally important literature across subjects so that the future generations may have an opportunity to study and learn from past works to embark upon a journey of creating a better future.

This book is a result of an effort made by Lector House towards making a contribution to the preservation and repair of original ancient works which might hold historical significance to the approach of continuous learning across subjects.

HAPPY READING & LEARNING!

LECTOR HOUSE LLP
E-MAIL: lectorpublishing@gmail.com